MY LIFE AS A
SIKH

FLEUR BRADLEY

45TH PARALLEL PRESS

Published in the United States of America by Cherry Lake Publishing Group
Ann Arbor, Michigan
www.cherrylakepublishing.com

Editorial Consultant: Dr. Virginia Loh-Hagan, EdD, Literacy, San Diego State University
Content Adviser: Molly H. Bassett, Associate Professor and Chair in the Department of Religious Studies
    at Georgia State University
Reading Adviser: Beth Walker Gambro, MS, Ed., Reading Consultant, Yorkville, IL
Book Designer: Jen Wahi

Photo Credits: © intek1/istock, cover, 1; ©Luciano Mortula – LGM/Shutterstock, 4; © Curioso.Photography/
    Shutterstock, 7; © AbhishekMittal/Shutterstock, 8; © Matt Hahnewald/Shutterstock, 10; © Siddharth Setia/
    Shutterstock, 13; © GUDKOV ANDREY/Shutterstock, 14; © sunil sonu art/Shutterstock, 16; © Sumit Saraswat/
    Shutterstock, 17; © lightlook/Shutterstock, 19; © Tinxi/Shutterstock, 20; © FeyginFoto/Shutterstock, 22;
    © Sukhvinder Saggu/Shutterstock, 24; © Falak0001/Shutterstock, 27; © Prabhjit S. Kalsi/Shutterstock, 28;
    © zixia/Shutterstock, 29; © Dean Drobot/Shutterstock, 30

45th Parallel Press is an imprint of Cherry Lake Publishing Group.

Library of Congress Cataloging-in-Publication Data

Names: Bradley, Fleur, author.
Title: My life as a Sikh / by Fleur Bradley.
Description: Ann Arbor : Cherry Lake Publishing, 2022. | Series: How the world worships
Identifiers: LCCN 2021039844 | ISBN 9781534199446 (hardcover) | ISBN 9781668900581 (paperback) |
    ISBN 9781668902028 (pdf) | ISBN 9781668906347 (ebook)
Subjects: LCSH: Sikhism—Juvenile literature. | CYAC: Sikhism—Essence, genius, nature—Juvenile literature.
Classification: LCC BL2018 .B73 2022 | DDC 294.6—dc23
LC record available at https://lccn.loc.gov/2021039844

Printed in the United States of America
Corporate Graphics

ABOUT THE AUTHOR:

Fleur Bradley is originally from the Netherlands. She likes to travel and learn about different cultures whenever she can. Fleur has written many stories for kids and educational books. She now lives in Colorado with her family.

TABLE OF CONTENTS

Did you know? The Golden Temple is covered entirely in gold foil. During the 1990s, the temple was renovated. Over 1,000 pounds (453 kilograms) of pure gold was used!

INTRODUCTION

Religions are systems of faith and worship. Do you practice a religion? About 80 percent of the world's population does. That's 4 out of 5 people.

Every religion is different. Some have one God. That's called **monotheism**. Other religions have multiple gods. This is called **polytheism**. Some religions have an **icon** instead of a god. An icon is an important figure. Sikhism, or Sikhi, is a monotheistic religion.

Sikhism is the world's fifth largest religion. About 90 percent of all Sikhs live in India. The other 10 percent live in the United States, Canada, and the United Kingdom. In the United States, less than 1 percent of the population are Sikhs.

Sikhs believe in one God. Sikhism is founded on the idea that good deeds are important. Good deeds lead to good **karma**. Bad deeds lead to bad karma. Karma means someone's acts in life.

Sikhs believe in **reincarnation**. Reincarnation is the rebirth of a person after death. **Mukti** is the only way to break the cycle of life, death, and rebirth. Mukti means closeness to God. It can be achieved through honest work, prayer, and giving to others.

Sikhism began in Punjab about 1500 CE. Punjab is in northern India. Sikh means disciple or follower in Punjabi. The founder of Sikhism was named **Guru** Nanak. Guru means spiritual teacher.

Guru Nanak was born into Hinduism. But he rejected the religion. He also studied other religions such as Islam.

Nanak rejected the idea that you have to fast or go on a pilgrimage. He believed that everyone is equal in God's eyes.

GOLDEN TEMPLE

The Golden Temple is the most important temple. It is located in Amritsar, a city in Punjab, India. It is surrounded by water that is considered holy. Sikhs sometimes bathe in it.

The temple has 4 entrances. This is to show that all are welcome.

There is a clock tower, a museum, and a langar. A langar is a community kitchen that serves free vegetarian meals to all. Langar is also the name of the meal being served.

Over the years, the temple has been destroyed by opposers of Sikhism. But it has always been rebuilt. Sikhs often make a pilgrimage to the Golden Temple.

Did you know? From birth, most Sikhs don't cut their hair. Hair is a symbol of respect and Sikh pride.

The first 10 gurus are called the Enlightened Masters. They were the ones who established and developed the religion. The fifth guru was Guru Arjan. He wrote the Sikh scriptures called **Guru Granth Sahib**.

The tenth guru created **Khalsa**. Khalsa is the Brotherhood of all Sikhs. The Khalsa follow strict guidelines called the Five Ks. They were considered soldier-**saints**. Saints are holy people. The Khalsa were ready to fight for their faith.

In 1966, the Indian government divided Punjab into 3 parts. They allowed the Sikhs to control only 1 of these parts. The Sikhs felt the boundaries were unfair.

Sikhs today practice their religion in different ways. At its core, Sikhism believes in helping the needy and doing good.

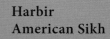

Harbir
American Sikh

CHAPTER 1

AN AMERICAN SIKH

My family and I have arrived at the **gurdwara**. A gurdwara is a Sikh temple. Today is an important day for me. It's my **Amrit Sanskar**. That's a ceremony to celebrate my commitment to Sikhism.

This ceremony is usually performed for adults. I'm honored to celebrate it so young. I'm only 15 years old.

"You look handsome, Harbir." My mother gives me a smile and removes some lint from my shoulder. I'm wearing the traditional white clothing and a turban.

"Thank you," I say. I'm a little nervous. But mostly I'm proud.

Is there a Sikh temple in your area? What activities and celebrations are held there?

My cousin Tanvir and his family arrive. Tanvir is also having his Amrit Sanskar today.

He hops out of the car and rushes to join me. "Dude, are you ready?"

I laugh. "*Dude*, yes," I say. Tanvir and I aren't just cousins. We're best friends too.

We go inside the gurdwara. Tanvir and I are no longer joking. This is a serious and important ceremony.

The 5 **Panj Piare** are waiting for us. They are initiated Sikhs who represent the 5 original Khalsa. They're dressed in orange and yellow.

The ceremony begins. The Panj Piare explain the Sikh principles we must observe. Then one recites sacred text. Another stirs the **amrit**. Amrit is sacred water, made with sugar.

Amrit Sanskar is an initiation into the Sikh religion. Can you think of other religions that have a similar ceremony? How is it different or similar?

Did you know? Hola Mohalla is a holiday that honors Sikh artists and warriors. The celebration includes sharing poetry and horse-riding competitions.

Tanvir and I get amrit poured in our hands. We drink it. Then amrit is sprinkled on our head and face.

We recite the **Mool Mantar** 5 times. Mool Mantar is the Sikh statement of belief.

At the end of the ceremony, we sing the **Anand Sahib**. It's a happiness hymn. Then, Tanvir and I get **karah parshad**. This is a sweet blessed pudding.

Now, we are officially Khalsa!

Did you know? Sikh women fought in battles alongside men. Sikhs believe women and men are equal. Mai Bhago was the first Sikh woman warrior.

Chapter 2
An Amrit Sanskar Celebration

I'm a little relieved the ceremony is over. My parents are proud. They take a moment to talk to my aunt and uncle.

Tanvir exhales in an exaggerated way. "Man, I'm glad that went well. I thought I was going to sneeze during the singing."

I nod. "It feels weird, being Khalsa now."

Tanvir agrees. "Yeah. I feel like I need to behave better."

"You? Behaving? Yeah, right," I joke.

Our mothers motion for us to join the family. "Let's go, boys," my mother calls.

My father says, "Now that you're Khalsa, we expect you to work 5 times as hard."

We all laugh.

There will be some celebration later. First, there is langar. Langar is a meal we prepare to feed the poor.

Every week, dozens of homeless people come to our Sunday langar. As Sikhs, our first duty is to perform **seva**. Seva is helping others. It's how Sikhs get closer to God.

Sikhism has an emblem called Khanda. It is made up of 3 symbols. The center has a double-edged sword and a chakram. This is a circular throwing weapon. It is surrounded by a 2-edged sword, for truth and justice. This symbol is often on a flag flown outside a gurdwara.

I help my father set up the tables in the community hall. Then we peel potatoes, wash cauliflower, and cut onions. Most gurdwaras have a kitchen. Langar is an important part of being Sikh.

Tanvir gives me a sad face as his eyes water from the onions. "You make me cry, Harbir."

I laugh and throw a towel at him.

"Stay out of trouble, boys," my aunt warns. Tanvir and I have a little history of trouble. Once we had a food fight before the langar cooking. Our mothers made us clean up. We were both grounded for weeks.

I say, "We will. We're Khalsa now."

She smiles. "Yes, you are."

Did you know? Some Sikhs eat meat, but most are vegetarian. They believe it is a personal choice. But all food served in the gurdwara is vegetarian.

HOLIDAYS

Sikhs follow their own calendar, called a Nanakshahi calendar. It is named after Guru Nanak. This means holidays don't always fall on the same dates. Here are some Sikh holidays:

Gurpurbs: throughout the year; festivals to commemorate important events surrounding gurus

Diwali: celebrated in October or November, called Festival of Lights, to remember the release of Guru Hargobind from prison in 1619

Hola Mohalla: celebrated mid-March, a festival with martial arts parades, music, and poetry readings

Vaisakhi: on April 13 or 14, celebrates Guru Gobind Singh performing Khalsa, or the establishing of the Sikh order, in 1699

Did you know? Not all gurus are human. Sikhs believe that their sacred text is also a guru. Their sacred text is called Guru Granth Sahib.

I put the potatoes on the stove. I think about being Khalsa. It comes with a lot of responsibility. I take my duties seriously, even if I do like to joke around with my cousin. We set up the serving tables once the meal is cooked. People are already lining up.

We serve good vegetarian food and no eggs. Keeping the body pure is part of Sikh beliefs.

Tanvir and I watch people eat. I feel proud to be a Sikh.

"Langar has to be the best way to spend a Sunday," I say.

Tanvir agrees.

Alisha
Indian Sikh

20

CHAPTER 3
A YOUNG SIKH IN INDIA

"It's okay, Junal," I say to my little sister. "Just stay close to me." Our family arrives at the Golden Temple in India. We are fortunate to live close. Today is April 14. This means it's Vaisakhi! This is the time Sikhs celebrate the New Year. It's my favorite time of year.

Many Sikhs walk around the temple. Some bathe in the surrounding water.

We go inside. The Guru Granth Sahib is bathed in milk during the service. It is our holy book. I thank God for everything. I think of Guru Nanak. He's our first guru. I'm thankful, especially today.

We sing at the end of the service. Then it's time to prepare for the celebrations.

I run ahead with Junal as we leave the Golden Temple.

"Alisha, Junal! Slow down!" Mother calls.

THE 5 Ks

Members who have entered the Khalsa observe the 5 Ks. These are physicals symbols of the Sikh faith:

1. Kesh: uncut hair

2. Kanga: a wood comb

3. Kara: a steel bracelet

4. Kacchera: cotton undergarments

5. Kirpan: a sword

Members of the Khalsa also wear a turban. These are mostly men, but sometimes women wear turbans as well. Often, women wear just a head covering. The turban is a sign of dignity, royalty, and self-esteem.

We do, but only a little. Junal is smiling. "Do you think we have enough flowers?"

I nod. We're making garlands with Grandma. "We bought enough to decorate the whole neighborhood!"

Junal and I finally slow down. There are already music performances around the Golden Temple. Junal does a little dance. I laugh. Grandma does too. She motions for us to move along. "We have work to do, girls."

She's right. For once, I don't mind. It's Vaisakhi!

Vaisakhi is a Sikh New Year's celebration. Think of how you celebrate New Year's Eve. How is the Sikh celebration the same as yours? How is it different?

Did you know? There are special performances during Vaisakhi. The Bhangra dance is one of them.

CHAPTER 4
A NEW YEAR'S CELEBRATION

My grandma, Junal, and I spend the rest of the morning making flower garlands.

We're still wearing our best dresses and head coverings. I have to be careful not to get pollen on my clothes.

"Which one is your favorite, Alisha?" Junal asks me. "I like the pink rose pedals."

"The orange marigolds are my favorite," I say. It's nice to sit and make garlands together.

We decorate outside when we're done. Then it's time to celebrate!

There is dancing in the street. I love it. I join in with Junal. She laughs and almost gets lost in the crowd. I keep an eye on her since I'm the oldest.

We watch the parade with Grandma. The Guru Granth Sahib is carried on a pillow. Vaisakhi is also celebrated to remember the founding of the Khalsa. Those are the 5 Sikh who are the origin of the Sikh faith.

"Let's go watch the kirpan fights!" Junal says as she pulls my arm. Kirpan fights are mock sword fights. They are performed to remember and celebrate the early Sikhs. Grandma comes along.

Look up "Vaisakhi Sikh holiday" on the internet. What do the celebrations look like? Is any of it similar to the way you celebrate?

SACRED TEXTS

Sikhism's sacred text is the Guru Granth Sahib. It is a collection of teachings from all the gurus, starting with Guru Nanak. Some are verses attributed to Nanak, while others are poems and hymns.

The teachings of Nanak focus on meditation, called *Naam japna*. Meditation means clearing your mind. It also tells Sikhs to earn an honest living, *Kirat karna*, and share with the needy, *vand chhakna*.

Did you know? Diwali is also celebrated by other religions! Hindus and Buddhists also celebrate Diwali.

Did you know? Similar to other religions, most Sikhs cover their heads. Men wear turbans. Women wear head scarves. But they can wear turbans, too.

There's music. We watch some of the performances together. At the end of the day, we eat karah parshad.

We get to stay up late to celebrate. In the evening, we light candles. There are fireworks too. Everyone is happy. Junal falls asleep on Grandma's lap.

I love Vaisakhi. It makes me proud and happy to be Sikh!

ACTIVITY

SEVA

Seva is an important part of Sikhism. Seva means doing something nice or good to help others.

TRY PRACTICING SEVA:

1. Alone or as part of a group, think of seva. What acts of kindness could you do?

2. Brainstorm a list of 5 small things you can do. They can be acts like holding the door for someone or saying something kind.

3. Now think of some bigger actions that take more effort. Could you volunteer for a day? Cook for your family? Help a friend study after school to pass a test?

4. Make a list of your seva actions, big and small. Check them off as you complete them.

5. How did these actions make you feel? Could you continue these acts of kindness?

TIMELINE OF MAJOR EVENTS

1469 CE: Guru Nanak, Sikhism's first guru, is born

1500: Guru Nanak founds Sikhism

1600: Guru Arjan, the fifth guru, works on the holy text Guru Granth Sahib

1606: Guru Arjan is killed for his faith

1619: Guru Hargobind is released from prison, which is celebrated during Diwali

1699: Tenth guru, Guru Gobind Singh, founds the soldier-saint order of the Khalsa Panth

1799: Indian prince Ranjit Singh establishes the Sikh Empire in Punjab

1849: British forces dissolve the Sikh empire

1919: A British general orders the mass killing of Indians in Amritsar massacre

1949: India becomes independent of Great Britain

1966: Sikh portion of Punjab is assigned

LEARN MORE

FURTHER READING

Hawker, Frances, and Mohini Kaur Bhatia. *Sikhism in India.* New York, NY: Crabtree Publishing, 2010.

Marsico, Katie. *Sikhism.* Ann Arbor, MI: Cherry Lake Publishing, 2017.

Self, David. *The Lion Encyclopedia of World Religions.* Oxford, UK: Lion Children's, 2008.

WEBSITES

BBC Bitesize—What is Sikhism?
https://www.bbc.co.uk/bitesize/topics/zsjpyrd/articles/zkjpkmn

Britannica Kids—Sikhism
https://kids.britannica.com/kids/article/Sikhism/353772

GLOSSARY

amrit (AM-ruht) sacred water made with sugar

Amrit Sanskar (AM-ruht sahn-SKAR) a ceremony to celebrate commitment to Sikhism

Anand Sahib (AH-nuhnd SAH-hib) a Sikh happiness hymn

gurdwara (GURD-wah-ruh) Sikh temple

guru (GUHR-ooh) spiritual teacher

Guru Granth Sahib (GUHR-ooh GRANTH SAH-hib) Sikh sacred text

icon (EYE-kahn) an important figure

karah parshad (KAH-ruh pahr-SHED) sweet pudding, sometimes blessed, given after ceremonies; also called prasad

karma (KAR-muh) the good or bad forces created by person's acts in life

Khalsa (KAHL-suh) brotherhood of all Sikh, originally soldier-saints

monotheism (mah-nuh-THEE-ih-zuhm) the belief in one God

Mool Mantar (MOOL MAN-tahr) Sikh statement of belief; introduction of Guru Granth Sahib

mukti (MUK-tee) closeness to God, believed in Sikhism to break reincarnation cycle

Panj Piare (PANJ PEE-ahr) initiated Sikhs who perform ceremonies

polytheism (PAH-lee-thee-ih-zuhm) the belief in multiple gods

reincarnation (ree-in-kar-NAY-shuhn) the rebirth of a person's soul into another being after death

saints (SAYNTZ) holy people

seva (SEH-vuh) doing good for others, believed to bring Sikhs closer to God

INDEX